MONTH-BY-MONTH
QUILT & LEARN
ACTIVITIES

25 Easy, No-Sew Quilting Activities for Reading, Writing, Math, Social Studies, and More

by Kathy Pike, Jean Mumper, and Alice Fiske

SCHOLASTIC
PROFESSIONAL BOOKS

NEW YORK • TORONTO • LONDON • AUCKLAND • SYDNEY
MEXICO CITY • NEW DELHI • HONG KONG • BUENOS AIRES

Cover design by **Gerard Fuchs**
Interior design by **Holly Grundon**
Edited by **Arianne Weber**

ISBN 0-439-23467-0

Copyright © 2002 by Kathy Pike, Jean Mumper and Alice Fiske
All rights reserved.
Printed in the U.S.A.
Published by Scholastic Inc.
1 2 3 4 5 6 7 8 9 10   40   09 08 07 06 05 04 03 02

To everyone whose "piece" is essential in providing a quality education to all students —
especially to Brenda McGuire, a parent and educational consultant, who has given
so much to the teachers and children at Cambridge Central School.

— K.P.

To my grandmother, Lovinia Mance Stedner, who taught me how to enjoy the
small things in life and showed me how to make the pieces fit together.

— J.M.

To Nan Banker, whose friendship, support, and encouragement are valuable pieces
in the "fabrics of my life."

— A.F.

We'd like to acknowledge the students at Cambridge Central School, Ostrander
Elementary School in the Wallkill School District, and Roxbury Central School
District whose work is featured in this book; the teachers whose efforts in "piecing
their students' education together" are greatly appreciated (Caroline Ashton, Pat
Baumann, Susanne Bischoff, Teddy Harrington, Barbara Johnson, Mary Laedlein,
Sue Sawyer, Melissa Skellie, and Karen Whitman); and our editors at Scholastic,
Liza Charlesworth and Kama Einhorn.

Contents

January

February

March

April

May

June

SECTION 3:
For Reference

Why We Use Quilts in the Classroom

Quilts are like families made of fabrics, pieced together with love and care. When assembling quilts, many individual pieces are joined to form the finished piece, often the result of many people working together. This is the perfect analogy for the picture of an ideal classroom—comprised of unique, individual children working together in a cooperative, collaborative environment.

Quilts seem to naturally belong in the classroom. Not only do they make wonderful interdisciplinary classroom themes, incorporating social studies, language arts, science, and art, they also conjure up images of home, warmth, and tradition. They have been an important part of America's heritage; stories about westward movement and slaves escaping to freedom have been recorded on quilts. Likewise, science and math curriculum comes alive with quilts, where nature scenes and math concepts are easily depicted. Quilts also provide authentic opportunities for children to use listening, speaking, reading, writing, and art in meaningful, purposeful ways as they research the contents or theme of the quilts, plan the quilts' construction, and work together to assemble the pieces.

How This Book Is Organized

Each section of this book will help you create a school year enriched with the beauty and educational benefits of quilt work.

Section I explores the use of quilts as an interdisciplinary unit. Included in this section are activities based on applicable literature listed in the bibliography (see page 40), samples of quilts inspired by other selected pieces of children's literature, and a few additional quilt projects. Patterns for many of these activities are available in the Reproducibles section (see page 46).

Section II describes how quilting can provide the structure or framework for an entire school year. Each month, students create a standard-sized quilt block, which is then assembled into a whole-class quilt. We include a description and illustration or photograph of a quilt, along with a student example of a quilt block. We also provide ideas for quilt variations, using different art forms and nontraditional quilt blocks.

The content of these monthly blocks can be based on the themes presented here, or can include information about the students themselves, their school work, class celebrations, or extensions of books you are reading in class. We have incorporated ideas for different monthly themes, and books to support them. The possibilities are endless! Don't forget to hang the finished quilts around the school, as space allows, to showcase your students' work. Ten generic quilt block patterns can be found in the Reproducibles Section (see page 46).

Finally, finish off the school year by letting children take home their very own quilts! After the completion and display of the June quilt, each student's blocks can be reassembled into individual quilts, or memory quilts, that are representative of the entire year. Directions for creating these quilts are found at the end of Section II (see page 38).

Section III contains in-depth bibliographies, helpful for enriching or extending the quilting activities, while the reproducible patterns assist you in recreating select designs.

Some Final Thoughts

A classroom is like a quilt, comprised of many children with different backgrounds, beliefs, and interests. Like the quilt blocks, each piece being an integral part of the whole, each child is a valuable part of the class community. We hope you enjoy exploring this further in your own classroom.

Remember...

The ideas presented in these sections are springboards for all kinds of classroom learning. You might use it as a guide for planning a year-long memory quilt, or use it to support your curriculum each and every month. Just remember that quilts join us together! Whichever way you decide to use this book, your students will benefit from the work and beauty they create together.

Quilts as a Thematic Unit

A quilt theme, similar to other themes you explore in your classroom, might be undertaken for a two- to four-week period. Introduce a variety of book- and art-related extension activities as well as a bulletin board featuring quilts created throughout the unit. Ideas for including all of this in your classroom follow.

Introducing a Quilting Unit

Introduce the subject of quilts on the first day of school. If possible, display some actual quilts, or let children bring in quilts from home. Then begin a discussion about the history and origin of each one. Encourage children to answer the following questions: Was the quilt in the family for a long time? Did someone special make the quilt? Is there a particular design in the quilt? Were some special fabrics used in making the quilt? Write down new vocabulary words, such as "heirloom," and discuss their meanings.

Continue enhancing the theme by displaying quilts, pillows, wrapping paper, notepaper, wall hangings, and toys in a special section of your room. Place books, magazines, and stationery featuring quilts in the writing corner.

Finally, incorporate quilt-related books into your read-aloud sessions. These read-alouds are nice springboards for many cross-curricular activities, as well as a continuing source of rich vocabulary.

The Quilting Bulletin Board

Create a bulletin board to feature children's quilting activities. You might display the many projects that children have completed over the course of the unit, so they can see how much they have accomplished!

Quilting Bulletin Board

DIRECTIONS

 1. Cover a bulletin board with the 8-inch paper squares.

 2. Give each student a 6-inch square for the first classroom quilt. Let children draw something that relates to a theme you have chosen, or allow them to choose one of their own.

3. Staple each block to an 8-inch square. The first classroom quilt is on display!

Materials

- 8-inch squares of bright construction paper for background
- 6-inch squares of construction paper
- markers or crayons

Quilting Concepts Across the Curriculum

Now that you have established quilting as an overall theme, you are ready to introduce it throughout the curriculum. Try to have an actual quilt to refer to in each curriculum area; it will help children apply the concepts you are covering.

Language Arts

Reading, writing, listening, and speaking fill the majority of time in the classroom. Using quilts as a theme gives you and your students many opportunities to talk, listen, read, and write for a variety of purposes. Children will talk and listen to their peers as they compare quilts, share quilt histories, and describe the quilts displayed in the classroom. They will read, listen to, and write quilt stories, and they will write captions for their pictures and directions on how to construct quilts. Before you are finished with the unit, children will have added new vocabulary to the class word wall and will have verbally mastered a description of quilt colors and shapes.

Social Studies

Young children spend a lot of time studying colonial life, the Pilgrims, families, farms, and communities, all topics easily depicted on quilts. As you cover these and other areas, use quilts or pictures of quilts to show what life was like then or what it is like now. To learn more about the process of quilting, show a video or invite a quilter to the classroom. You might take a field trip to a museum or to a fabric store to see the fabrics and some of the tools used in quilting.

Math

Children can learn to identify colors, shapes, and patterns in a quilt's design and then construct their own quilts using simple mathematical patterns, such as AABB, ABCABC, ABABAB, and so on. These quilt patterns can be constructed from Unifix cubes, tiles, colorful rubber bands and Geoboards, or one-inch squares of colored construction paper. Introduce the concept of symmetry by

having children find examples of symmetrical designs in the quilts. Children can then create their own symmetrical design by pasting pumpkin or heart shapes onto a quilt block. See an example of a kindergarten heart quilt above.

Science

When looking at the quilts and pictures of quilts, children might find, list, and perhaps illustrate how nature is represented through the pictures and designs. They might also create quilt blocks for science topics such as the seasons, weather, or rocks. See an example of a second-grade science quilt at left. Furthermore, children can learn how fabrics and dyes are made and can experiment with making their own dyes from onion skins and berries.

10

Using Quilt Literature

> **C**omplement your quilting unit with applicable children's books. We provide titles and story summaries to get you started, as well as activities or projects to try. Other titles are listed in the bibliography.

The Quilt
BY ANN JONAS
A child's new quilt comforts her at bedtime.

No Dragons on My Quilt
BY JEAN RAY LAURY
When a young boy is afraid of going to bed, he is comforted by a quilt his grandmother made for him.

After reading either or both of these books, begin a discussion about bedtime fears. Follow up by constructing bedtime quilts. The quilts can be made with fabric or cardboard and decorated to resemble a quilt. You might also place them on beds made from cardboard boxes.

Box Beds
DIRECTIONS

 1 Use the template to create bed boards cut from cardboard or foam trays, and glue them onto both ends of a box.

 2 Paint the boxes or cover with fabric.

 3 Have students place squares of fabric on the beds. A rectangular shape can serve as a pillow.

Materials

- boxes (cigar, tissue paper, shoe, and so on)
- foam trays or cardboard
- fabric or construction paper; other materials for decoration
- quilt block template (reproducible 1)
- glue
- crayons or markers

The Rag Coat

BY LAUREN MILLS

A girl proudly wears her new coat made of clothing scraps to school, but the other children make fun of her until they learn about the history of the scraps.

After reading this story, students can construct their own rag coats. They can paste these coats onto the coat template (reproducible 14), and then write a brief description about what the scraps represent in their own life.

The Whispering Cloth

BY PEGI SHEA

A young girl in a Thai refugee camp recalls a story from her past to create her own pa'ndau.

Tar Beach

BY FAITH RINGGOLD

Based on the author's quilt paintings, this story tells about a young girl who dreams of flying above her Harlem home, claiming all she sees for herself and her family.

Children can use these two stories to create their own storytelling quilt. Instead of sewing together pieces of fabric to tell stories, use pellon cut into desired shapes and displayed on flannel boards. Children can use any story to create this unique quilt square, including those you make up as a class!

The Kissing Hand

BY AUDREY PENN

A young raccoon is reluctant to go to kindergarten until his mother shares a secret way for him to carry her love along.

What a perfect book to read to children who are going to school for the first time! After reading the book and discussing those first-day jitters, children can make the kissing hand quilt.

Kissing Hand Quilt

DIRECTIONS

 1 Have children trace their hand on a sheet of construction paper. Help them cut out their handprints and paste them onto the middle of the template.

 2 Cut out the template. Children can either draw small hearts in the center of their hand or place a heart-shaped sticker in the center. Their names can be written somewhere in the quilt block. They can then decorate their squares.

3 Arrange the quilt blocks in an attractive quilt pattern on a bulletin board (use decorative paper for a border).

More Projects With Quilts

There are many other quilting projects that will enhance your curriculum, from quilt stationery to plastic bag refrigerator memo holders.

Quilt Stationery

Students can invent their own pattern, or select a pattern related to a unit of study. For example, while learning about the ocean, each student can draw an ocean animal quilt block, which can then be reduced and pasted on paper (reproducible 3) to form the border.

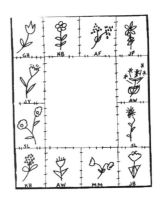

Quilt Bookmarks

To create quilt bookmarks, give students rectangular pieces of paper and have them design four of their own quilt blocks on four separate squares of paper. Then students paste the quilt blocks to the bookmark. Remind students to write their name on the back of bookmark in case it gets lost!

Quilt Place Mats

Decorate place mats with quiltlike borders, made from individual children's squares. If possible, laminate the place mats for durability.

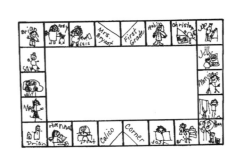

Quilt Picture or Storybook Frames

You can create quilt-bordered picture frames in three different ways:

- Glue 3-inch wallpaper squares along the edge of a piece of posterboard or oaktag. The size of the posterboard can vary, but it is best to give each child a standard size-for example, a 12-inch square. Each child decorates a square.

- Each child can design his or her own quilt block, which can then be reduced to the desired size on the copy machine. Each child then receives a copy of his or her classmates' blocks, colors them, and glues them onto the edge of the posterboard frame. This is similar to the border created for the quilt stationery.

- Have children color 3-inch versions of standard quilt patterns and glue them along the edge of the frame.

Inside their frame, students can glue a piece of their writing, a scene from a storybook, pictures of the class during the quilt unit, and so on.

"My Own Fabric" Quilt

Quilters often use fabrics that are special to them or to those who will receive the quilt as a gift. This tradition is significant in the read-aloud books *Crazy Quilt*, *My Grandmother's Patchwork Quilt*, *A Book and Pocketful of Patchwork Pieces*, *The Patchwork Quilt*, *Owen*, and *The Quilt*. After reading one or more of these books and discussing the story, tell children that they will be making a quilt from material that is special to them. Send home a note explaining the project to parents, and request that each child bring in a piece of fabric that is meaningful to them.

Remember to bring in fabrics that are meaningful to you as well. As you display your pieces of fabric, explain how they fit together to tell a story about your life.

After children have brought in their fabric, attach the materials to a 6-inch posterboard square. Display the squares on a bulletin board. Stories about the fabric memories can be written and displayed nearby. Later, use the quilt squares and stories to create a class book and place it in the class library.

Refrigerator Memo Quilt

Create a plastic bag quilt for children to put on their refrigerators. Place student writing, artwork, or information about homework, needed supplies, important dates, and so on, in the individual plastic bags.

DIRECTIONS

 1   Arrange four plastic bags on a flat surface in two rows of two. Tape the individual bags together; make sure that the openings are not taped shut.

 2   Attach two small magnets or pieces of magnetic tape to the back of the quilt.

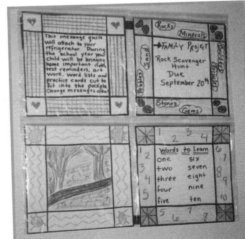

 3   Place small pieces of oaktag inside each plastic bag to keep the bag stiff.

 4   Place the information or student work to be showcased in the bags. The contents of the bags can be changed throughout the year.

Materials

- resealable plastic sandwich bags (4 per student)
- tape
- small magnets
- pieces of cardboard, posterboard, or oaktag (cut to fit inside bags)
- student artwork, student writing, or teacher notes

Quilt Checklists

As early as kindergarten, children learn to use daily checklists as organizational tools. They use them to see their progress, keep track of tasks to be completed, and follow directions. By using a quilt block as the checklist, children will also end up with a piece of artwork! Use reproducibles 2 and 4 to create these sample checklists.

Ending the Quilting Unit

To end the unit, plan and host a quilting bee or a patchwork party, or prepare a quilt-hanging ceremony. Children can make patchwork place mats and use homemade quilt stationery to write invitations. If there are a number of student-constructed quilts on display, guests can vote for their favorite quilt. Post the "winner" in a prominent place outside the classroom for all to enjoy.

Other Ideas for Making Quilts

Here are still more quilts to make during the school year:

- ABC Quilt
- Poetry Quilt
- Family Quilt
- Multicultural Quilt
- Our Class Quilt
- Postcard Quilt
- Authors or Illustrators Quilt

September

Creating a "Getting to Know You" quilt is an excellent way to begin the school year. It also might be the first time your students have created a quilt block, so encourage them to have fun and be creative! Each student decorates a quilt block square, and the finished blocks are joined together to form one large class quilt. This is a nice feature for open houses and during American Education Week.

Materials

- quilt block templates (reproducible 2 or 5)
- construction paper
- photographs (if possible)
- markers or crayons
- glue
- posterboard

Getting to Know You: A Classmates Quilt

DIRECTIONS

1. Have students decorate their template with either photos or drawings of themselves.

2. Encourage students to write information in the block about their hobbies, families, pets, homes, and so on. Don't forget their names!

3. Cut out the quilt blocks and glue them onto construction paper. Glue the quilt blocks onto the poster board. Combine into one large class quilt.

Mural Quilt

Help children develop a sense of their own abilities and accomplishments by creating a quilt based on the classic story *The Little Engine That Could*. After reading this book aloud and discussing the themes of self-worth and confidence, students can create a mural entitled "I Know I Can, I Know I Can." Construct a train from construction paper, with enough cars to hold each classmate, and glue onto a long strip of mural paper. After children draw their self-portraits, cut them out and insert each one into a car.

Apple Prints

DIRECTIONS

Since apples are plentiful, have students make quilt blocks using apple halves and paint!

 1   Ahead of time, cut apples in half so that the star design is visible.

 2   Give each child several apple halves and a small amount of paint.

 3   Children dip an apple half into the paint and then press the apple onto the quilt block. They may make just one apple print or create a design using several apple prints.

 4   Children can glue apple seeds around the block to create a border. Arrange all squares to form a quilt!

Other September Themes

Apples
Shapes
Our Community
Pets

Materials

▪ apple halves
▪ paint
▪ quilt block template (reproducible 6)
▪ construction paper

October

Because the harvest is a time for people to gather their crops, this is a perfect time to focus on gathering favorite stories! Children can illustrate a scene on a quilt block or help create a basket of books.

Materials

 quilt block template (reproducible 4)

 construction paper

markers or crayons

glue

photocopies of book covers (reduced)

 basket shapes (cut from construction paper)

 posterboard

A Harvest of Books Quilt

DIRECTIONS

1. Have students glue a basket shape to the center of the block.

2. Have students cut out photocopies of the book covers and place them in the basket, so that the titles and cover illustrations show. All students should then decorate the rest of the block with their name and anything else related to their chosen books.

3. Glue the blocks onto construction paper and attach them to posterboard.

4. Combine to create a class quilt!

Envelope Quilt

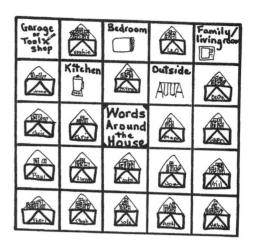

Since envelopes are essentially small containers, they are perfect for using on quilts to hold information. To create an envelope quilt, attach envelopes, flap side out and open, to the center of a quilt block, or arrange on a quilt background, such as posterboard or a bulletin board. Have children decorate the envelopes. Inside the envelopes, children can insert 3" x 5" cards or slips of paper containing poems, thoughts, ideas, or summaries of their favorite books.

Thumbprint Pictures

DIRECTIONS

 1 Provide children with a quilt block and ink pads in various colors.

 2 Demonstrate how to gently press a finger or thumb into the ink pad and then make a finger mark on the quilt square. Encourage children to then add details to the prints to make people, animals, flowers, and even objects used for the harvest.

 3 Glue the block to construction paper. Combine to create a class quilt!

Materials

- quilt block template (reproducible 6)
- construction paper
- stamp pads
- crayons or markers

Other October Themes

Families
Leaves
Fire Safety
Pumpkins

November

Harvest celebrations such as Thanksgiving are excellent opportunities for children to explore what they are thankful for.

"We Are Thankful for..." Quilt

DIRECTIONS

1. In the top triangle of the X, have students write "I am thankful for..." Then have them decorate the other three triangles with something they are thankful for in their lives. Encourage them to label each illustration.

2. Have children cut out the square and then glue it onto the quilt block. Make the class quilt by gluing the finished blocks onto posterboard or attaching them to a bulletin board.

Materials

 quilt block template (reproducible 7)

 markers or crayons

glue

posterboard

Ribbon Quilt

Use extrawide ribbon or old, donated neckties to create a unique way to display quilts. Cut strips of the material to desired lengths and attach them to a bulletin board. Attach students' quilt blocks to the ribbons in a staggered pattern.

Hand Art

Hand-tracing is a popular art activity with young children—and it makes wonderful designs for quilt blocks. Try this activity with your class:

DIRECTIONS

 1 Demonstrate how to trace your hand on a sheet of paper. Have students do the same on the quilt block.

2 Show children how to spread their fingers apart, to make a turkey or several people, or keep their fingers close together, to make a flag or an ear of corn.

 3 After tracing, children can add details using crayons or markers.

 4 Glue the finished block onto construction paper. Combine to create a class quilt!

Materials

- quilt block template (reproducible 8)
- construction paper
- crayons or markers

Other November Themes

Native Americans
Colonial Times
Dinosaurs

December

Young children love show and tell! Now that children have grown more comfortable with school and with each other, this is a wonderful time for them to begin sharing special items from their homes. On a designated day, have children bring in a favorite keepsake to show to the class and to illustrate for their quilt block.

Materials

 quilt block template (reproducible 9)

 construction paper

■ markers or crayons

■ glue

Favorite Keepsakes Quilt

DIRECTIONS

1. In the top triangle, have students write "My Keepsake" and illustrate a special keepsake. In the bottom triangle, they write about their keepsake object and then add its name. Encourage children to make the pictures really colorful!

2. Glue the quilt blocks onto construction paper, and then attach them to a bulletin board to create a class quilt!

Paper Plate Quilt

Use colorful paper plates to display children's quilt blocks! After children have drawn their keepsake on their quilt block, glue each block to the center of a paper plate. Then arrange the paper plates on posterboard or a bulletin board.

Stained Glass Pictures

Prior to beginning this activity, show students examples of art made with tissue paper, such as paper flowers. Follow with a discussion of the textures and patterns they saw. Remind students that tissue paper is thinner than regular paper and therefore more delicate, so they should take care in handling it! Please note: Leave adequate drying time for this project.

DIRECTIONS

 1 Ahead of time, precut pieces of tissue paper in various shapes and sizes. Help students paint a very thin layer of liquid starch on their quilt blocks.

 2 Have students choose pieces to place on their quilt block. Encourage them to layer different colors for a special effect.

 3 Let dry to a shiny glasslike finish. Display all squares together as a giant stained glass window!

Materials

- quilt block template (reproducible 8)
- tissue paper (in different colors)
- liquid starch
- paintbrushes

Other December Themes

Catalog Fun
Preparing for Winter
Healthy Bodies

January

This is the month in which we honor the hopes and dreams of Dr. Martin Luther King, Jr. It's also an ideal time for children to explore and express their own hopes and dreams for the future. On cloud-shaped pieces of paper, they will record their dreams and hopes and then glue them to the sky.

Materials

- quilt block template (reproducible 5)
- light blue and light purple watercolors
- construction paper
- water
- paintbrushes
- white lined paper
- markers or crayons
- glue

"I Have a Dream" Quilt

DIRECTIONS

 1. Using watercolors and water, have students paint a watercolor wash of blue and purple all over the quilt block.

 2. On the lined paper, students can draw and cut out cloud shapes. Then have them write on the lines their hopes and dreams for the future. Glue the cloud to the middle of the diamond shape on the template.

 3. Cut out the template and glue it onto the construction paper.

 4. Attach the finished blocks to a bulletin board.

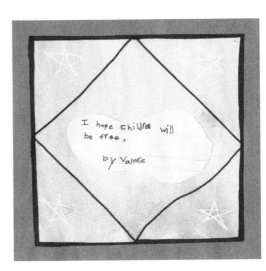

Vinyl Shade Quilt

To construct this quilt, unroll an entire vinyl shade and lay it on a flat surface. Using a yardstick and permanent marker, create a grid on the shade to outline each quilt square. Be sure to leave a border around each square. Glue the squares onto the shade, using glue made for vinyl material. If preferred, children can draw directly on the shade with permanent markers. Hang the shade anywhere. Remember, storing the shade is a snap!

Watercolor Haiku

Experimenting with paint can be a wonderful learning experience. Using a variety of watercolor paints, children can create a design or picture on their quilt block square. Watercolor wash is a simple process used to achieve a soft colorful painting.

DIRECTIONS

 1 Photocopy the quilt block template onto the heavy paper. Instruct children to wet the paper with their brushes, taking care not to use too much water.

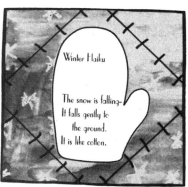

 2 Dip the brush first in water and then in paint. Have children touch the brush to the paper where there is water, causing the paint to spread. Continue the process until the paper is filled with colorful blends.

 3 When dry, details can be added with permanent marker or cut paper. Add a Haiku written on mitten-shaped white paper!

Materials

- quilt block template (reproducible 2)
- heavy white drawing paper
- watercolor paints in various colors
- paintbrushes

Other January Themes

Winter Fun
Snow
Bedtime Dreams
Weather

February

The 100th day of the school year is a big event, and many students eagerly mark off each day in anticipation. Many classrooms plan celebrations or projects around the occasion, and quilting is a wonderful way to celebrate!

Materials

- quilt block template (reproducible 10)
- markers or crayons
- glue

100th Day Quilt

DIRECTIONS

 1 Have students decide how to show 100 of any object (dots, small stickers, popcorn kernels, and so on) on their squares.

 2 On the template, have students write the number 100 in the upper-left-hand box, and the word "days" in the upper-right-hand box. They can then use the other two boxes to note what they are counting, such as 100 buttons or 100 popcorn kernels.

 3 In the open space, they can illustrate what they are counting or glue on the objects themselves.

 4 Glue the squares onto a quilt block. Arrange the blocks together on a bulletin board.

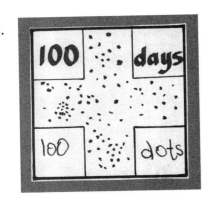

Magnetic Quilt

Create a quilt for the 100th day of school that is quite magnetic! Give each child a jar top or lid from canisters or canning jars. On a piece of paper cut to fit the lid, children write the numeral 100 in a creative way. Glue the drawings onto the lids, and attach a small magnet or a piece of self-stick magnetic tape to the back side. Arrange the jar tops on a cookie sheet or other magnetic surface decorated to look like a quilt (use peel-away shelf liners).

Collage

The art of collage is explored in wonderful children's books by Eric Carle, Leo Lionni, and Denise Fleming. You might begin this activity by reading one of these books and discussing the special look of the art on each page.

DIRECTIONS

 1. Ahead of time, collect various collage materials and place them in accessible containers.

 2. After children decide what to illustrate, have them arrange the materials on the quilt block. Encourage children to experiment with overlapping the materials, for an interesting effect.

 3. Glue the finished blocks to construction paper and combine to make a class quilt.

Materials

- quilt block template (reproducible 8)
- construction paper
- photographs, magazine pictures
- wallpaper, fabric, wrapping paper, tissue paper
- small objects (seeds, leaves, coins, cereal pieces)
- glue

Other February Themes

Black History
Valentine's Day
Presidents
Money

Other 100th Day Quilt possibilities include:

100 Reasons We Like Grade ____
100 Ways to Be a Friend
100 Tips (advice) for ____
100 Book Characters

March

Get your kids excited about reading for Read Across America Day, which happens this month! On this day, everyone is encouraged to spend time reading and doing fun activities associated with books. You might create activities that involve books by the beloved Dr. Seuss—he was born in March!

Materials

- quilt block templates (reproducibles 5 and 11)
- construction paper
- markers or crayons
- glue

Storybook Quilt

DIRECTIONS

 1 Let students select their favorite storybook.

 2 Using markers, crayons, and cut paper, they can depict a scene in the center of the quilt block, adding pertinent information about the characters and plot along the borders or in the corners.

 3 Glue the finished pieces to construction paper and combine on a bulletin board.

Shape Quilt

Have fun with shapes by making a quilt that isn't rectangular or square! Instead, create a quilt that takes on the shape of something children are reading this month. For example, if you are reading Dr. Seuss's *Cat in the Hat*, you might create a quilt in the shape of a hat. Draw an outline of the hat on a piece of posterboard or mural paper. Have students illustrate a scene from the book on quilt blocks, and then arrange them in a quiltlike fashion inside the hat.

Cotton-Swab Painting

Young artists often enjoy experimenting with different art tools. Try using cotton swabs instead of paintbrushes to design quilt blocks, and watch how creative kids can be!

DIRECTIONS

 1   Demonstrate the effect of using a cotton swab instead of a paintbrush. Show children how to use the tip of the swabs to create a picture made mostly of circles.

 2   Once students have decided on an illustration, have them dip their cotton swab into paints or touch the stamp pads and create a picture.

3   Encourage students to illustrate the middle section of the quilt block, leaving the two other sections to write their name and add a sentence or two about what they created.

Other March Themes

Spring
Animal Babies
Wind

Materials

- quilt block template (reproducible 12)
- cotton swabs
- various colored paints or stamp pads

April

As you welcome spring to your classroom, celebrate all that is new on the earth around you by creating a commemorative Earth Day quilt. You might begin by making a list of all the different ways we can help the earth: protect endangered animals, recycle materials, conserve energy, reduce pollution, clean up the ocean, rivers, or waterways, save the rain forest, and so on.

Materials

- quilt block template (reproducible 11)
- construction paper
- markers or crayons
- adhesive bandages
- glue

Earth Day Quilt

DIRECTIONS

 1 Have students think of ways to illustrate a healthy earth. Children can draw or find a picture of the earth and place it in the middle of the quilt block.

2 Around the border, they can write what we need to do to keep the earth clean, such as recycle, protect animals, and clean the oceans.

 3 Students can attach an adhesive bandage to the surface of the earth and add the label "Heal the Earth" to the illustration.

4 Glue the finished blocks to construction paper, and then attach to a bulletin board covered in green construction paper.

Plastic Bag Quilt

This quilt is special because it can be used as a holder. All you need are posterboard, large resealable plastic bags, and tape (for attaching the bags to posterboard). The content of this quilt can be varied on a regular basis, depending on what you are working on in class. Simply insert children's work into the bags!

Crayon Resist

Creating crayon-resist pictures is a fun way to combine drawing and painting!

DIRECTIONS

 1 Demonstrate how to draw a picture first with crayon, and then paint over the crayon with the watercolors.

 2 Show children how the areas without crayon will absorb the paint, while the areas with crayon will "resist" it.

 3 Children can choose to draw a picture of their own. Wait until squares are dry before displaying them as a class quilt.

Materials

- quilt block template (reproducible 8)
- crayons
- watercolor paints

Other April Themes

Endangered Species
Plants
Recycling
Poetry

May

As the school year draws to a close, both teachers and students reflect on the days that have passed. Memorable moments may focus on a field trip, a guest speaker, a schoolwide celebration, or a special friend. This month, create a quilt that is a collection of your students' memorable moments.

Memorable Moment Quilt

DIRECTIONS

1. Have students decide which memorable moment to illustrate on a quilt block.

2. Have children use actual photographs or crayons or markers to illustrate that moment on the block.

3. They can add captions to the pictures, describing the moment and how they felt.

4. Glue the finished quilt blocks to construction paper, and attach the finished squares to posterboard or a bulletin board.

Materials

 quilt block template (reproducible 2)

 photographs

 markers or crayons

 glue

Other May Themes

Butterflies
Mother's Day
Folktales

Frame Quilt

Because memorable moments are "snapshots" of a day or an experience, creating quilted picture frames is a perfect way to showcase these moments forever.

DIRECTIONS

 1 Begin with a square sheet of paper and mark the midpoints of the four sides.

 2 Fold each corner to the center point, using the marked midpoints as a guide for each fold.

 3 Fold each point under until it reaches the inner edge fold. Glue each edge of the frame down and have students attach photos or illustrations.

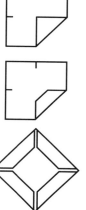

Sponge Painting

Here's another great way to paint pictures—without a paintbrush!

DIRECTIONS

 1 Ahead of time, cut sponges into a variety of shapes.

 2 Demonstrate how to dip the sponge shape into paint, creating a picture or interesting design. Once dry, students can draw a picture with markers or crayons.

June

I t's time to say good-bye to a wonderful school year! This is a perfect time to make a quilt that features the whole class.

Materials

 quilt block template (reproducible 13)

 construction paper

class photo

 markers

 glue

Autograph Quilt

DIRECTIONS

1 As a class, select a photograph that you like best. Be sure everyone is visible!

2 Glue the picture to the center of the quilt block.

3 Have each student sign his or her name around the border of the block.

4 Cut out the template. Make copies and glue them to pieces of construction paper. Distribute the copies so that every student has one. Then let each student decorate or color his or her template to take home.

5 Display the original quilt block in a prominent place.

Floor Tile Quilt

Because floor tile patterns resemble quilt blocks, they are ideal to use for quilting purposes. After purchasing a floor tile from a home supply store, glue the class picture in the middle and have children sign their names in permanent marker around the picture. If other classrooms in the school create a quilt block, you can put them all together to create a school quilt!

Favorite Story Quilt

Use felt or pellon to create fun, colorful quilt blocks. (With pellon, children can draw right on the surface, color it, and cut it.)

DIRECTIONS

 1 Show children some samples of felt or pellon illustrations.

 2 Demonstrate how to color on the pellon using crayon or markers. Encourage children to make different shapes, representing their favorite story which they will then cut out.

 2 Glue a piece of felt on the template, as a background. After the shapes have been cut, glue them onto the felt background to create the picture. Children may also choose not to glue their illustrations so they can be used for storytelling purposes.

Materials

- quilt block template (reproducible 8)
- pellon or felt
- felt for background
- crayons or markers
- glue

Other June Themes

Ocean
Vacation Fun
Transportation
Summer Safety

N ow that the school year is over, you have at least ten full-size quilts! While your class has enjoyed making and displaying them, it is time to take them apart and send children home for the summer with their own quilts. The memory quilt is created by gathering each child's quilt blocks and making them into one special quilt. Follow these instructions for creating memory quilts for every student in your class.

Memory Quilt

DIRECTIONS

1   Separate the ten quilts that you have made throughout the year, separating the quilt blocks into piles according to the students who created them.

2   Return the piles of quilt blocks to the students who created them. Each child should have the ten quilt blocks that he or she created during the year.

Materials

- 10 quilt blocks (September–June)
- 2 blank quilt blocks for each child
- crayons, markers, or paints
- tape

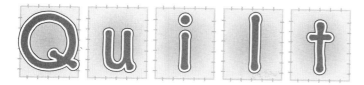

☀ **3** Give each child two blank quilt blocks to decorate and add their name and grade to.

☀ **4** Have children arrange the 12 quilt blocks in an interesting pattern. Then tape the quilt blocks together on the back.

☀ **5** When the year has ended, send each child home with their memory quilt as a memento. It is a wonderful keepsake to share with parents and friends!

For Reference

Refer to the bibliographies below for help in locating quality quilting literature.

Quilting Books

Blia Xiong. 1989. *Nine-in-One, Grr! Grr! A Folktale From the Hmong People of Laos*. San Francisco: Children's Book Press.

When the great god Shao promises Tiger nine cubs each year, Bird comes up with a clever trick to prevent the land from being overrun by tigers. Illustrated with colorful paintings depicting the applique story cloths of the Hmong.

Bolton, Janet. 1994. *My Grandmother's Patchwork Quilt: A Book and Pocketful of Patchwork Pieces*. New York: Doubleday.

Alternating pages describe a young girl's life on a farm and how she constructed a quilt to capture memories of her life. There are ten quilt squares included for readers to create their own quilt.

Brumbeau, Jeff. 2000. *The Quiltmaker's Gift*. Duluth, Minnesota: Pfeifer-Hamilton Publishers.

A generous quiltmaker agrees to make a quilt for a greedy king under certain conditions, which causes the king to have a change of heart.

Coerr, Eleanor. 1986. *The Josefina Story Quilt*. New York: Harper & Row.

While traveling west with her family in 1850, a young girl makes a patchwork quilt chronicling the experiences of the journey—and reserves a special patch for her pet hen, Josefina.

Cole, Barbara. 1990. *Texas Star*. New York: Orchard Books.

Although Papa grumbles about his family not needing another quilt, he is only too happy to use it after the quilting bee.

Dorros, Arthur. 1991. *Tonight Is Carnival*. New York: Dutton.

A little boy prepares for carnival time in Peru.

Edelman, Marian Wright. 1998. *Stand for Children*. New York: Hyperion Books for Children.

A version of the speech delivered at a rally at the Lincoln Memorial is presented in this powerful picture book. Multilayered quilts illustrate the inspiring words.

Ernst, Lisa. 1983. *Sam Johnson and the Blue Ribbon Quilt*. New York: Lothrop, Lee, & Shepard Books.

While mending an awning, Sam discovers that he enjoys sewing the patches together, but he meets with scorn and ridicule when he asks his wife if he could join her quilting group.

Flournoy, Valerie. 1985. *The Patchwork Quilt*. New York: Dial.

This book tells the story of a contemporary African-American family. Using scraps cut from the family's old clothing, a young girl helps her grandmother and mother make a quilt that tells the story of her family's life.

Fowler, Christine. 1998. *Shota and the Star Quilt*. New York: Zero to Ten Ltd.

Set in Minneapolis, this modern story examines an age-old theme—the triumph of love and friendship over power and greed. A complete Lakota translation is included.

Friedman, Aileen. 1995. *A Cloak for the Dreamer*. New York: Scholastic.

When a tailor asks his three sons to make a cloak for the archduke, the third son's design reveals his desire to travel the world.

Grifalconi, Ann. 1990. *Osa's Pride*. Boston: Little, Brown.

Osa's grandmother tells her a story about the sins of pride and helps Osa gain a better perspective on what things are really important.

Guback, Georgia. 1994. *Luka's Quilt*. New York: Greenwillow Books.

Luka is initially disappointed in the quilt her grandmother made for her, but eventually the two settle their differences.

Hopkinson, Deborah. 1993. *Sweet Clara and the Freedom Quilt*. New York: Knopf.

A young slave stitches a quilt with a map pattern that guides her to freedom.

Johnston, Tony. 1985. *The Quilt Story*. New York: Putnam.

A pioneer mother stitches a quilt for her daughter, and years later another mother patches it for her little girl.

Kinsey-Warnock, Natalie. 1988. *The Canada Geese Quilt*. New York: Dodd, Mead.

Worried that the coming of a new baby and the seriousness of her grandmother's illness will change her family's life on a Vermont farm, a young girl uses her artistic ability along with her grandmother's knowledge to make a special quilt.

Kuskin, Karla. 1994. *Patchwork Island*. New York: HarperCollins.

A mother stitches the varied topography of their beautiful island into her patchwork pattern while making a quilt for her child.

Levitin, Sonia. 1996. *A Piece of Home*. New York: Dial.

A little boy moves from Russia and takes along his great-grandmother's special blanket.

Love, Anne. 1995. *Bess's Log Cabin Quilt*. New York: Holiday House.

With her father away and her mother ill, a young girl works hard making a log cabin quilt to save the family farm.

Lyons, Mary. 1993. *Stitching Stars: The Story Quilts of Harriet Powers*. New York: Charles Scribner's Sons.

Quilts of family history, Bible stories, and folktales are featured in this biography of an African-American quilter.

McKee, David. 1968. *Elmer, The Story of a Patchwork Elephant*. New York: McGraw-Hill.

All the elephants in the jungle are gray except Elmer, who is a patchwork of brilliant colors. Then one day he gets tired of being different.

Mills, Lauren. 1991. *The Rag Coat*. Boston: Little, Brown.

Minna proudly wears her new coat made of scraps of clothing to school, where the children make fun of her until she tells them the stories behind the scraps.

Parton, Dolly. 1994. *Coat of Many Colors*. New York: HarperCollins.

A poor girl is happy with her coat of many colors, made from rags by her mother, because despite being ridiculed by other children, she knows the coat was made with love.

Paul, Ann. 1991. *Eight Hands Round: A Patchwork Alphabet*. New York: HarperCollins.

This book introduces the letters of the alphabet with names of early American patchwork quilt patterns and explains the origins of the designs.

Paul, Ann. 1996. *The Seasons Sewn: A Year in Patchwork*. Orlando, Fl.: Harcourt Brace.

Pioneer life in the nineteenth century is depicted through the quilts that people created.

Polacco, Patricia. 1988. *The Keeping Quilt*. New York: Simon & Schuster.

A homemade quilt ties together the lives of four generations of an immigrant Jewish family, a symbol of their enduring love and faith.

Rinaldi, Ann. 1994. *A Stitch in Time*. New York: Scholastic.

This historical novel is set in Salem, Massachusetts.

Rinaldi, Ann. 1995. *Broken Days*. New York: Scholastic.

Walking Breeze's mother tries to unite her daughter with her family, but a cousin does everything to make her feel unwelcome. A sequel to *A Stitch in Time*.

Ringgold, Faith. 1991. *Tar Beach*. New York: Crown Publishers.

Based on the author's quilt painting, this story tells about a young girl who dreams of flying above her Harlem home, claiming all she sees for herself and her family.

Ross, Kent and Alice Ross. 1995. *Cemetery Quilt*. Boston: Houghton Mifflin.

When her grandfather dies, a young girl doesn't want to go to his funeral until her grandmother shares the family's cemetery quilt.

Shea, Pegi. 1995. *The Whispering Cloth, A Refugee's Story*. Honesdale, Pa.: Boyds Mills Press.

A young girl in a Thai refugee camp finds the story within herself to create her own pa'ndau.

Smucker, Barbara. 1995. *Selina and the Bear Paw Quilt*. New York: Crown Publishers.

When her Mennonite family moves to Canada to avoid involvement in the Civil War, young Selina is given a special quilt to remember the grandmother she left behind.

Zagwyn, Deborah. 1990. *The Pumpkin Blanket*. Berkeley, Calif.: Celestial Arts.

A little girl sacrifices her beloved blanket to save the pumpkins in the garden from frost.

Teacher Resources

Baycura, Debra. 1990. *Patchwork Math 1 and Patchwork Math 2*. New York: Scholastic.

Bernard, Robin. 1999. *Crayon Projects: 25 Instant Activities That Bring Out the Creativity in Every Kid*. New York: Scholastic.

Bonica, Diane. 1989. *Hand-Shaped Art*. Torrance, Calif.: Good Apple.

Bonica, Diane and Kathy Devlin. 1997. *Cooperative Quilts: Classroom Quilts for the Entire School Year*. Torrance, Calif.: Fearon Teacher Aids.

Buchberg, Wendy. 1996. *Quilting Activities Across the Curriculum*. New York: Scholastic.

Cigrand, Mariann and Phyllis Howard. 2000. *Easy Literature-Based Quilts Around the Year*. New York: Scholastic.

Evans, Joy and Jo Ellen Moore. 1992. *How to Teach Art to Children*. Monterey, Calif.: Evan-Moor.

Flores, Anthony. 1983. *From the Hands of a Child*. Torrance, Calif.: Fearon Teaching Aids.

King, Rendy and Maureen King. 1995. *Quilt Connections*. Greensboro, NC: Carson-Dellosa Publishing Company, Inc.

Kohl, Mary Ann and Jean Potter. 1998. *Global Art: Activities, Projects & Inventions From Around the World*. Beltsville, MD: Gryphon House.

Pike, Kathy and Jean Mumper. 1998. *Books Don't Have to Be Flat!: Innovative Ways to Publish Students' Writing in Every Curriculum Area*. New York: Scholastic.

Pike, Kathy, Jean Mumper, and Alice Fiske. 2000. *Teaching Kids to Care and Cooperate: 50 Easy Writing, Discussion & Art Activities That Help Develop Responsibility & Respect for Others*. New York: Scholastic.

Wilmes, Liz and Dick Wilmes. 1993. *Paint Without Brushes*. Elgin, Ill.: Building Blocks Publication.

Wilmes, Liz and Dick Wilmes. 1997. *Easel Art*. Elgin, Ill.: Building Blocks.

Zimmerman, Susan. 1996. *Quilts: A Thematic Unit*. Huntington Beach, Calif.: Teacher Created Materials.

Web Sites to Visit

www.quiltmakersgift.com
www.quilt.com
www.womenfolk.com
www.quilttownusa.com

Reproducible Student Pages

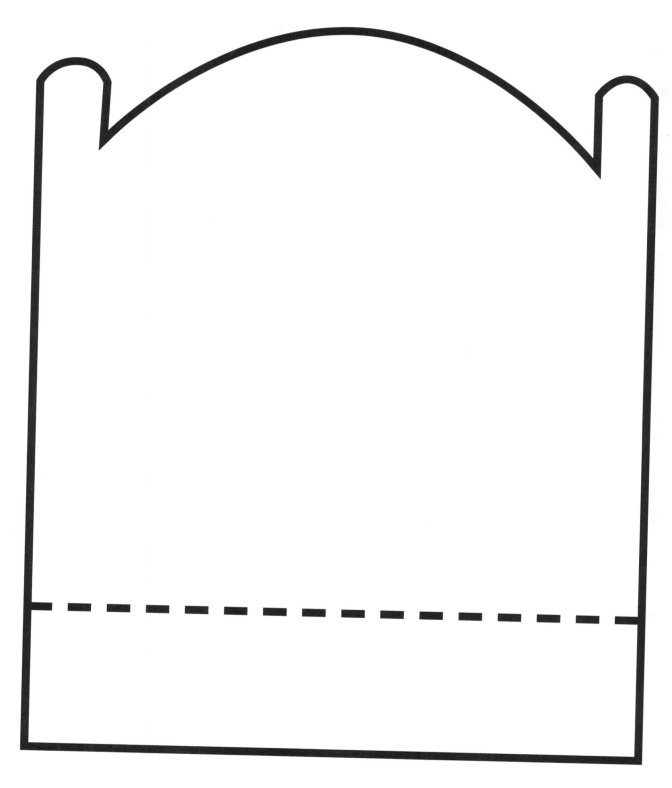

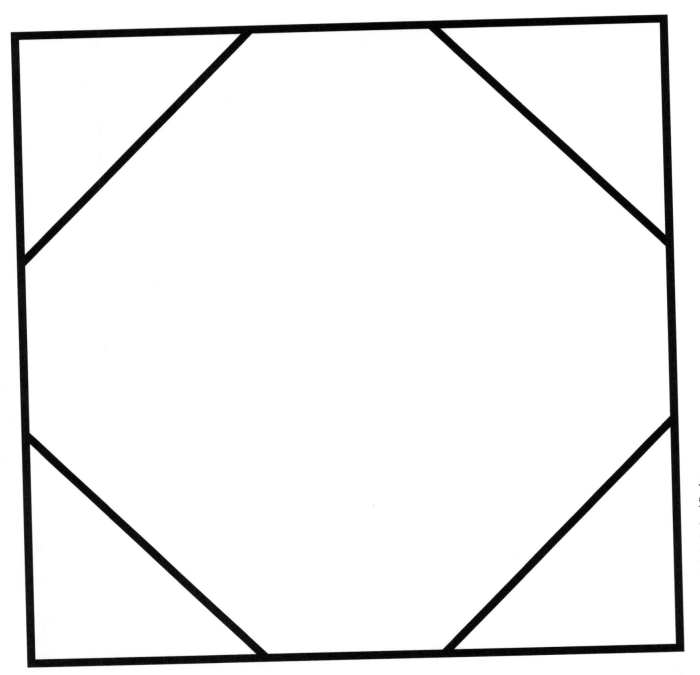

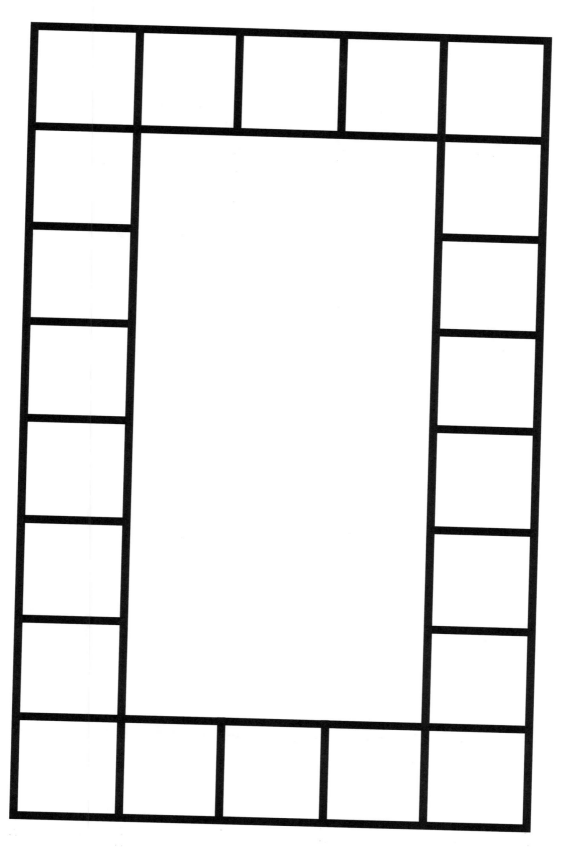

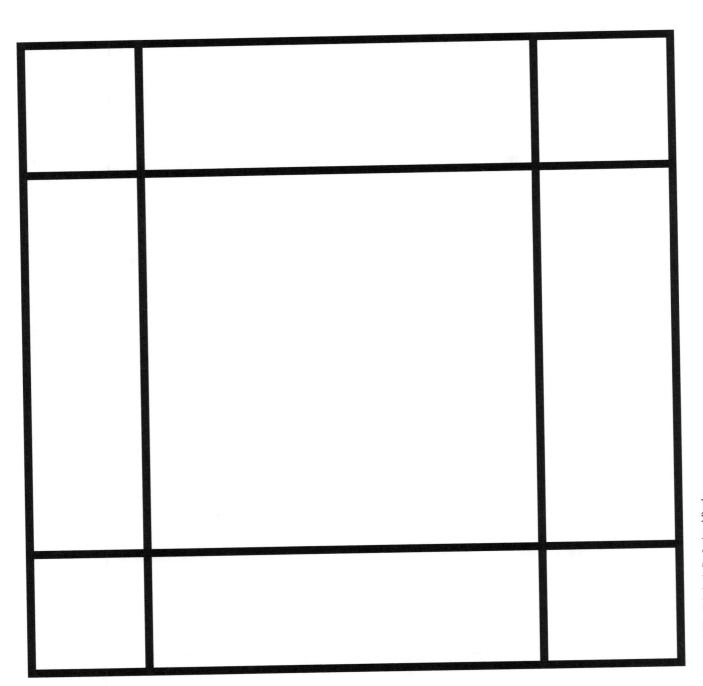

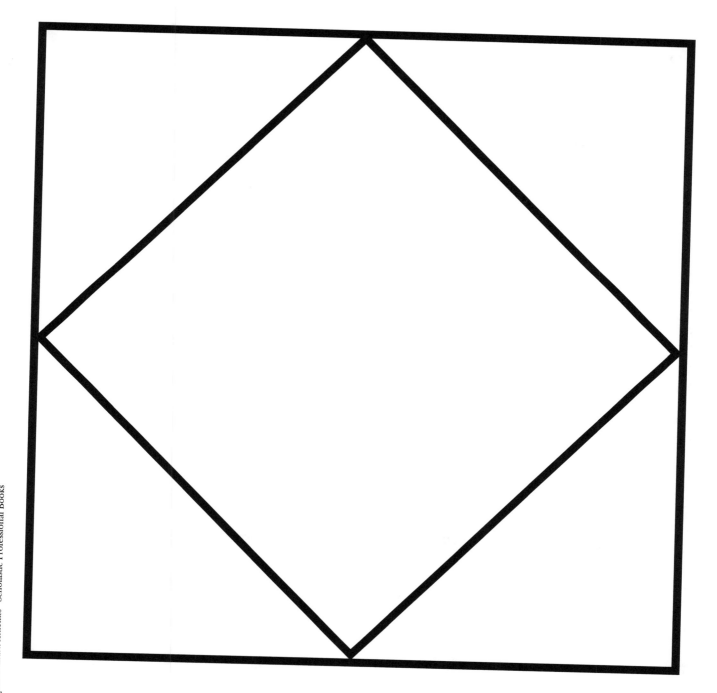

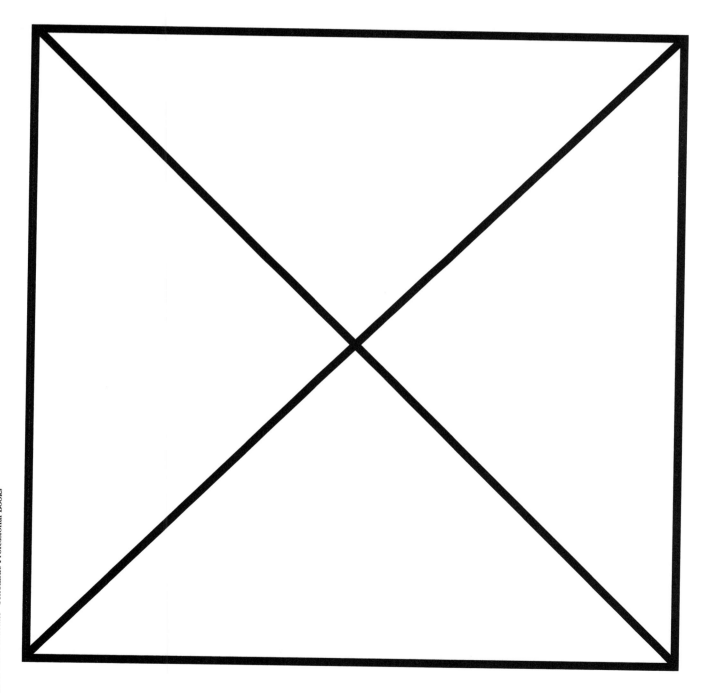

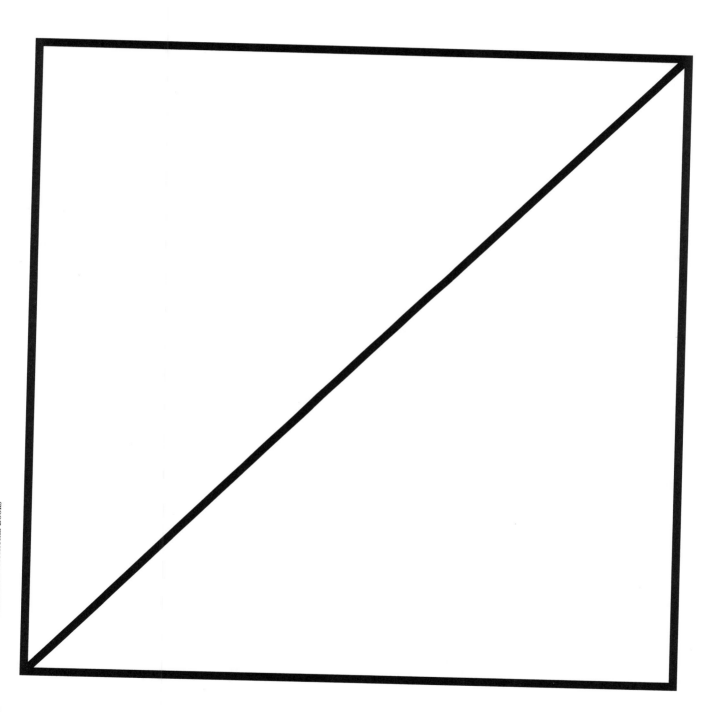

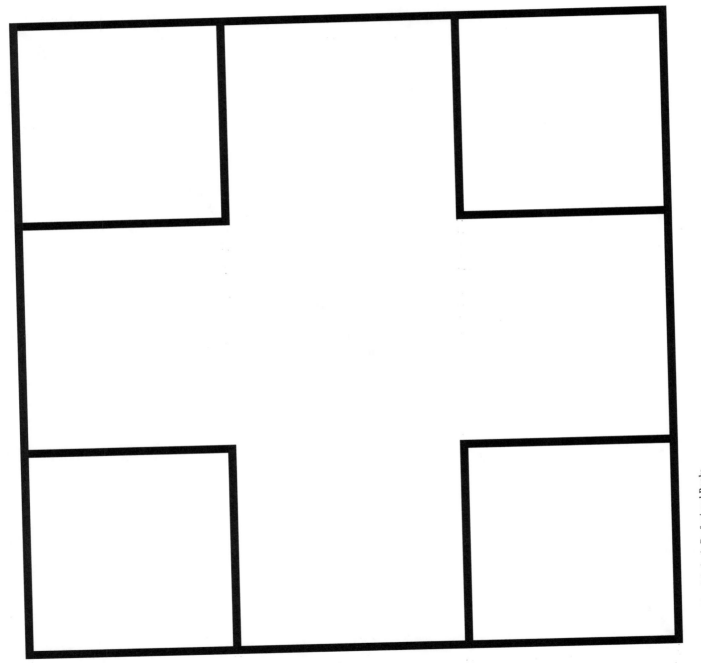

Month-By-Month Quilt & Learn Activities Scholastic Professional Books

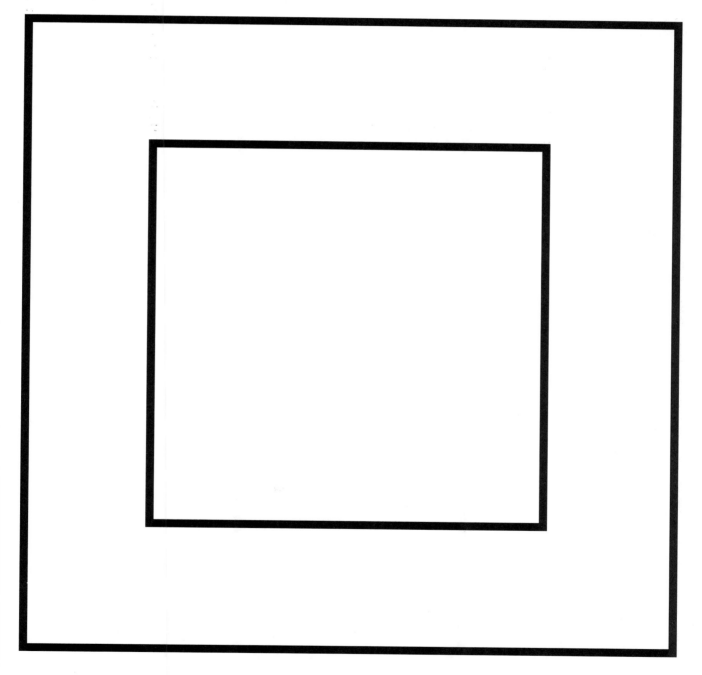

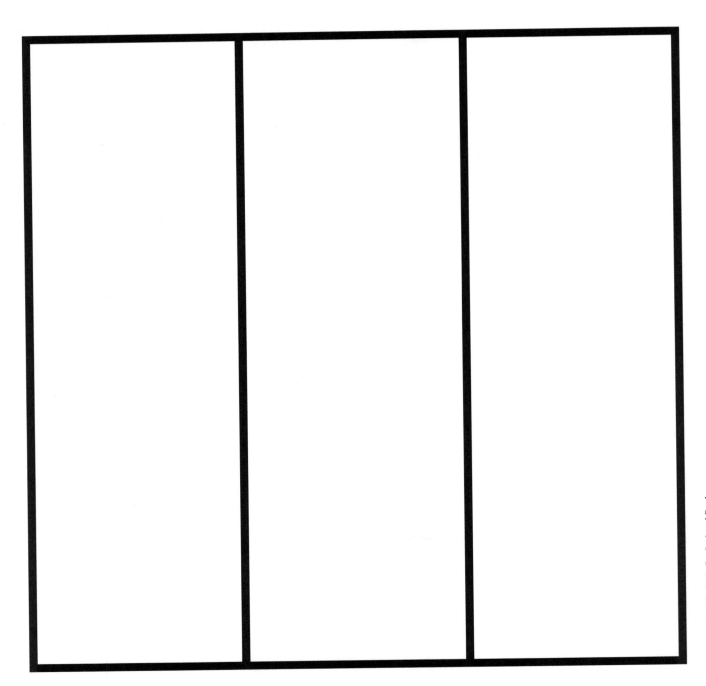

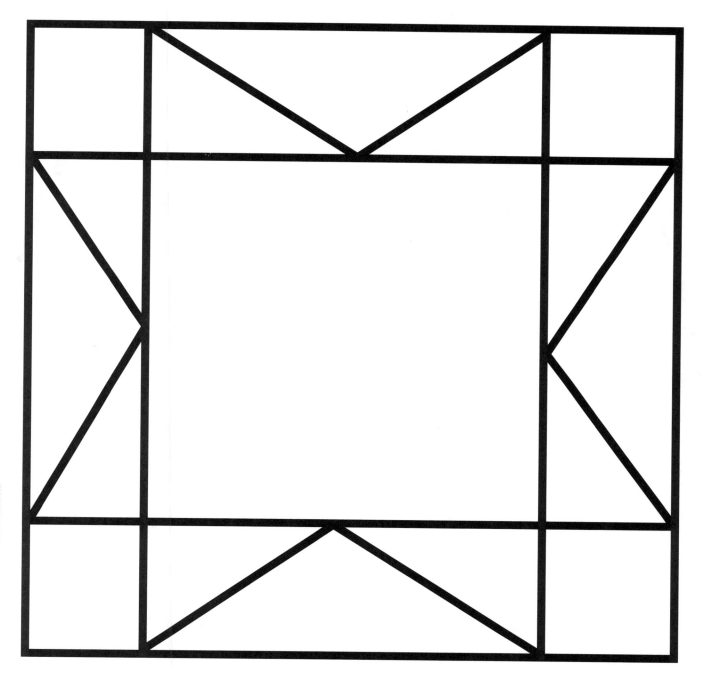

Notes

Notes

Notes

Notes